Becoming Daddy's Little Girl

Overcoming Rejection, Releasing Abandonment, and Growing Closer To God

Tonja L. Davis

BECOMING DADDY'S LITTLE GIRL. Copyright © 2021. Tonja L. Davis. All Rights Reserved.

Printed in the United States of America.

No portion of this book may be reproduced, stored in a retrieval system, or transmitted in any form or by any means, except for brief quotations in printed reviews, without the prior written permission of DayeLight Publishers or Tonja L. Davis.

Published by

DAYELight
PUBLISHERS

ISBN: 978-1-958443-44-6 (paperback)

Scripture quotations marked (NLT) are taken from the Holy Bible, New Living Translation, copyright © 1996, 2004, 2007 by Tyndale House Foundation. Used by permission of Tyndale House Publishers, Inc., Carol Stream, Illinois 60188. All rights reserved.

Scripture quotations marked "KJV" are taken from the Holy Bible, King James Version (Public Domain).

I dedicate this book to my daughters, Jasmine, Ashley, and Donalyn. The privilege and honor of being your mother was another experience God used to help me understand a Father's love for me. The thought that He could love me so much more than I could ever love Him wowed me and gave me an awareness of the vastness of His love for me.

In honor of my mother, Queen Esther Dantzler. I am because you were. Through this work, God will continue to extend your legacy of servanthood. I love you, Momma.

Acknowledgments

Thanks to my daughter, Ashley D. Davis. Your selfless giving of your time and talents has helped make this season effortless. I love you, baby girl. The legacy continues through you.

To New Home Family of Churches: You are intricately interwoven into the core foundation of what I have become. I will forever love you and your place in my process.

R.C. Blakes, Jr.: words cannot express the value of your presence over the years that have brought me to my transformation. I thank God, often, for seeing fit to bring you into my life and my spiritual walk as Pastor, Brother, and now Spiritual Father.

Thanks to Crystal Daye, you were a God-sent. I have been down this publishing road before, but when God maneuvered you into my publishing journey, He sent me exceedingly abundantly more than I could ask or think was possible. I have grown so much in the confidence of what God can and will do with this project.

Table of Contents

Acknowledgments .... *v*

Introduction *9*

Chapter 1: Everybody Has A Story 11

Chapter 2: My Soul's Search 15

Chapter 3: Meeting Daddy 19

Chapter 4: Becoming Who I Was 23

Chapter 5: First Things First.. 27

Chapter 6: In Daddy's Presence 33

Chapter 7: Why Did I Want To Be A Daddy's Little Girl 39

Chapter 8: Self-Proclaimed Or Authentic 43

Chapter 9: What Is A Daddy's Little Girl 47

Chapter 10: The Benefits Of Being A Daddy's Little Girl 53

Chapter 11: A Daddy's Little Girl In Her Daddy's Presence............. 57

Chapter 12: A Daddy's Little Girl Out Of Her Daddy's Presence 61

Chapter 13: Running The Family Business 67

About the Author *97*

Introduction

I must admit, the phrase "God's Timing" has never gone over well with me. I had challenges with the ability to wait. Patience was far removed from my life. I smile when I think about all the times impatience ruled, but that would be another book.

As I sit here to pen this, I am incredibly grateful for the time God has taken me through to get to this point. Oh, the wisdom I have gained over the years. That wisdom is poured into the pages of this book to empower you to identify, shed, discover, reveal, embrace, walk out, and eventually encourage.

As you become empowered on your journey through these pages, you will be able to empower others.

Be empowered. Be encouraged.

Chapter 1
Everybody Has A Story

For years, I have always said, *"Everybody has a story."* As a writer, teacher, and producer, I have passionately believed that. To write a piece for someone, I would immediately ask the question, *"So, what's your story?"* I had to know their story. Their story became my inspiration for the product I would create for them.

Recently, sitting at a meeting with an image consultant, I realized that I believed *"Everyone has a story,"* but not me. The consultant was presenting some work she had done for a recent client to give me a visual of what my outcome could look like since the client and I were both writers. I was impressed. This writer had finished her book on coming out of alcoholism, sold over one hundred pre-orders, and was getting herself out there as a public speaker. The consultant had done well by her. She then told me to get my information to her as soon as possible. I paused and then looked up at her. At that moment, I felt so helpless; I felt like a hypocrite.

For years, I had been creating God-inspiring products from the stories of so many people, but right then, at that moment, I did not have a story. I could not think of one thing that was the focal point of my love for God. The only thing I managed to tell her in our meeting was that if people went to all my social media pages, they would see that I was about "Faith" and "Family." What? If that was someone's response to me after my question, I would tell them, *"Sweetheart, that's your image. What is your STORY?"*

I teach middle school English/Language Arts; the entire curriculum is about teaching the stories. In the Ray Charles movie, my favorite line was when Jamie Foxx (Ray Charles) said he loved country music because *"They tell a story."* That is the same reason I love country music; THEY TELL A STORY. It is always about *"The Story"* for me. So, why in that moment did I not have one?

A story has a beginning, middle, and end, but it also has a point. Otherwise, why write it? What was the point of that author's book? Her point was to tell others how she overcame alcoholism in hopes of helping someone struggling with the same addiction or any addiction for that matter. Why would someone write a book on being delivered from prison? Answer: to show God's delivering power. Why would someone write a book on a total recovery from breast cancer? Answer: to show God's healing power. Why would someone write a book on going from extreme poverty to being a wealthy business owner? Answer: to show that God is a provider. Do you see my point? All of these "books" (*stories*) have a point. So, sitting there with the consultant, I had no focal point; therefore, I had no story.

Luke 7:47 (NLT) reads, *"I tell you, her sins-and they are many-have been forgiven, so she has shown me much love. But a person who is forgiven little shows only little love."* Those were Jesus' words in answer to the thought a Pharisee had about Him allowing the sinner woman to anoint His feet. Jesus was saying if a person is forgiven of a lot of things, that same person will love God a lot. But if a person is forgiven little, then that person will only love God a little. Years ago, when I read that scripture, I interpreted it to mean there was "big sin" and "little sin." So, I thought those who were forgiven of a "big" sin like alcoholism, drug abuse, or a crime that placed them in prison, led them to love God a lot. So, what is the deal with my love for God? I really love God a lot, although He did not have to forgive me of any of those listed sins. What "*big*" sin did God forgive me of that makes me love Him so much? In the years of my spiritual growth, I came to understand the truth of that scripture. The truth is, there is no "*big*" sin or "*little*" sin; sin is sin to God. Being forgiven of a crime against another person is no greater than being forgiven of gossiping or taking a pen off a desk without the owner's permission. Both actions are considered a sin in God's eyes, and He does not like either one. He considers both to be equal offenses to His loving ways, so if there is no such thing as a "*big*" sin and a "*little*" sin, then why do I love God so much? I believe when I find that answer, I will find "***my story***."

GET OUT YOUR JOURNALS:

What is your story? What would you tell someone if they asked about your life?

Chapter 2
My Soul's Search

The turning point of my relationship with God took place a few days before December 13, 1991. I was married, living in New Orleans, Louisiana, and raising a beautiful little girl named Jasmine. We will get back to that, but first, I need to give you a little history. I was born and raised in South Carolina. My mother was a strong parent. As a single mother, she raised three boys and one daughter. I learned a lot from my mother. However, I did not realize just how much I was learning in the moments and years I was growing up. The older my children got, the more I heard and saw how much of my mother's life and ways had been transferred to me. When scolding my children, the words or phrases I would say to them were the same phrases and words used by my mother. When making certain decisions or responding to certain situations, it would be like an immediate journey back in time, and I would be "*a fly on the wall*" watching my mother deciding and responding the same way. I did not cherish the lessons I had gleaned until after her passing.

My mother insisted that we attend church every Sunday. Even if she could not go, we still had to. A skating rink was the hang-out place for the middle and high schoolers from the surrounding neighborhoods. Every Sunday night, that was the "*thing*" to do. In our house, whenever you acted as if you did not want to go to church, my mother's standing response was, "*If you plan to go to that skating rink tonight, you better plan to go to church.*" Another way she would say it was, "*If you're too sick to go to church, you better be too sick to go to that skating rink later on.*" She meant every word of it too, so if you planned on going skating that evening, whatever was "*ailing*" you at the moment about going to church, the best thing to do was just "*suck it up*" and get dressed. Therefore, I went to church on a regular basis while growing up, but I remember my attendance was out of mere duty or blackmail.

I was just an audience member paying attention to the "*show*" going on around me. From the "*show*," I developed a sense of belief in "*The God.*" "*The God*" was who you prayed to when things went bad. "*The God*" lived in the sky, and His home was called heaven. "*The God*" put Earth together and could still control it if He wanted to. "*The God*" had rules He expected you to follow, just like my mom. "*The God*" had a Son named Jesus who died on the cross for our sins, so He was a Father. That is probably why He had rules; EVERY parent has rules. "*The God*" was also called "*Heavenly Father*" because He was everyone's Father at church and all of us were His children. I got a sense of all this through growing up and attending church, but I also got a sense of being far, far away from "*The God.*" I heard people say they knew Him, and I wanted to know Him too. I heard people say, "*Get close to God,*" and I wanted to do that, but how? Did I have to die and go to heaven to get close to "*The God?*" There had to be another way, but I did not know how.

This turning point I mentioned at the beginning of this chapter began with the sincere search to be satisfied inside. I felt I needed to be whole inside my mind, heart, or both, if they were two different things. Although I was living in this obvious physical world, I felt empty inside. I distinctly remember saying to the air, "*I want to begin going *to church because I WANT to, not because I'm supposed to."* Then, I looked up in that same air and said, *"God, I want to know You're real."*

Now, I can go into the details of the turning point. I was upstairs in our apartment, praying in my daughter's room. The memory of those moments is vivid even to this day. There, sitting on the floor, head bowed down, I picked up that conversation again, and with tears in my eyes, I began to speak my heart. My words were, *"Lord, I want to know You are real. Growing up, I never got the chance to be "Daddy's Little Girl." How can a father leave his only little girl? Why didn't he love me enough to stay? Why didn't he love me enough to make me feel special and loved? Every little girl wants to be "Daddy's Little Girl." Since You are our heavenly Father, that means You are "Daddy." So, can I be Your "Daddy's Little Girl?"* Nothing happened; no earth trembling and no lightning flashing. There was just silence and the noise of my continuous tears and sniffling. I felt really silly. I just asked an invisible God if I could be His *"Daddy's Little Girl."* How crazy was that, right? I wiped my eyes, cleaned my nose, and got up off the floor. As I took a couple of steps to walk out of the room, I paused to look back at the spot on the floor where I poured out the true inner desire of my heart to somehow still be *"Daddy's Little Girl,"* even if it is to an invisible God. I felt really silly; I even spoke it, *"Silly Tonja."* Then I turned and left the room.

It was a secret conversation with God, so I did not have to face any embarrassment when I left the room. It was a secret conversation; therefore, it was easy to paste the smile on my face and act as if nothing was yearning on the inside of me. It would not be difficult to act as if I was strong and had it all together. No one would understand my desire to be a little girl even though I was a grown woman, not to mention a grown woman with a child. But there I was, going on with life as usual, yet harboring that delicate but screaming desire to be embraced, nurtured, and loved by a father. I desired it from a Father who is invisible. How is that supposed to happen? Unknowingly, I had made the step to find out how. That day, in my daughter's bedroom, was the asking, seeking, and knocking mentioned in *Luke 11:9-10* and *Matthew 7:7*-8. That day was the beginning of the answers to my soul's search and desire.

GET OUT YOUR JOURNALS:

Have you experienced your soul searching for something more? What were your thoughts? What steps did you take to act on those thoughts?

Chapter 3
Meeting Daddy

I always knew that a prophet was a man who God chose, by the Holy Spirit, to communicate to His people, but I thought they ceased to exist after Jesus. I never thought much about a prophet in my day and time. When I first came to the New Home Ministry and heard about Prophet Blakes, I thought that was just a title name, such as "Reverend," "Pastor," or "Elder." Then I heard him being referred to as "*The Prophet.*" My interest arose, and I started wondering how this man came to be called "Prophet Blakes." They told me, "*Things happen in his church*"; "*God tells him things to tell people*"; "*He prophesies about people*"; "*He is so anointed, that he can just touch you and the Spirit of God will work.*" I kept hearing persons repeat those statements.

Time after time, the stories were the same and became even more wondrous to me. For a while, I was nervous about attending "*The Temple.*" It was called that, not because it was the name of the ministry, but because of its historic structure. After some time into my Christianity, I built enough confidence to finally decide to visit "The Temple" for a mid-week service. I had never been up close and personal to God's wondrous works, so all of that "*laying on of hands*" was new to me. The only place I had ever seen it was on television, and I was always told, "*Don't believe everything you see on T.V.*"

It was Thursday night, and I was on my way to *"The Temple."* I was not nervous, just curious about what would take place there. The service began as expected; it was very orderly, spiritual, and uplifting. The sermon was next; it was wonderful and enlightening. Something about that service was just for me. I was so caught up in this anointed man and what he had to say that even when he told us to turn to our neighbours, I could not take my eyes off him. To add to that, he walked the aisle a little during his sermon, and his eyes kept meeting mine. I turned to my co-worker/friend and said, *"I think this is my night. Do you see how he keeps looking at me?"* She nodded.

After the sermon, he started to prophesy, and I thought, *"Wow, this is just like on T.V."* Then, as if to test his validity, not out of disbelief but curiosity, I thought, *"Lord, tell him something about me. Let me know something."* I thought the Lord would reveal something trivial about me to him. This was just my thought; I did not think it would really happen.

I looked down distractedly at my feet as I listened to him go on. Then he was silent. When I looked up, he was looking at me. "Get up, Get up," he said. I sat there stunned! *Was he really talking to me?* I felt paralyzed, motionless, almost as if I was standing on the sidelines watching this moment take place. Still looking at me eye to eye, he said, "Come here and just give me a hug." After he said those words, something in me just knew he was directing his attention and words specifically at me. But, still stunned, I sat there motionless.

I wanted to move, but the shock of it all gripped and strapped me to my seat. Suddenly, I began to feel like the cushion under me started to rise slowly until I was on my feet. It was as if someone had squared out the section of the bench space I was sitting on and had a crank attached to the under seat. They then turned the crank to lift me up from the seat because I was too shocked to move, but, of course, that was not what happened. I give credit to the Holy Spirit for lifting me up.

After the Spirit lifted me up, I made my way to the person I thought was Prophet Blakes. When I made my way out of the row and into the aisle, he had moved away from my row of seats. As I walked towards him, I no longer saw Prophet Blakes; instead, I was walking towards my heavenly Father. The closer I stepped towards Prophet Blakes, the cloudier his area became. I kept going towards where I knew he was standing. Suddenly, it felt like I slipped into an atmosphere of cloud and glory. I opened my arms to give Prophet Blakes the hug he requested, but it was not him. God had taken a few minutes out of His busy schedule to come down and take the form of flesh to let one of his children know the answer to a deep and troubling question in her heart; that form He used was the form of Prophet Blakes.

As he/He placed his arms around me, it was not just a human hug; I felt a total wrap of warmth and security. I really felt as if I was hugging my heavenly Father, and He was hugging me back. I just wanted to hug him/Him more and more. I could have stayed there all night. Along with the hug, I heard Prophet Blakes saying, "You are going through something that no one knows about. Not even those close to you." That statement hit my heart so strongly; I knew what the "*something*" was. No one else knew what this '*something*' was. I felt I could not tell anyone because they would consider me to be silly, childish, or even crazy. I told myself no one would understand, so how did this man know? I only talked about that '*something*' with God, my heavenly FATHER.

Finally, it was time to let go. As much as I did not want to let go, I made my way back to my seat and pulled myself together. When I looked at the man again, I saw Prophet Blakes, and I began to reflect on what had just happened to me. As I watched him "work" his church, the word "amazing" came to my mind. He was truly an anointed man. Now I know why he was referred to as "The Prophet."

IN HONOR OF PROPHET ROBERT CHARLES BLAKES, SR
Inspired by a genuine Holy Ghost Experience
December 13, 1991

That encounter with Prophet Robert C. Blakes, Sr. was how God answered my soul-searching question that delicate night. That Holy Ghost encounter was the beginning of the rest of my life, learning my identity as *"Daddy's Little Girl."*

GET OUT YOUR JOURNALS:

Write about a time you believe you had an encounter with God. Do you believe that encounter was connected to your soul search?

Chapter 4
Becoming Who I Was

How can you *become* who you already *are*? That is only possible if you had no idea who you really are. When I met "*Daddy,*" I realized I did not know who I was. I did not know who I was because I really did not know who He was. Living as someone else's child or under someone else's influence causes you to conform to the person you think you are. That conforming process is based on what you live and what you are told every day. As you grow, your surroundings, life, and lifestyle determine your mindset. That mindset controls your decisions, beliefs, and speech. Therefore, you look, walk and talk just like your environment. Without another component or factor to influence, alter or challenge that existing mindset that has developed as a result of your surroundings, life, and lifestyle, you simply become a product of your environment. Your mind has been set to that standard; hence the word "*mind…set.*"

I had a mindset. Growing up, I became a product of my environment. I believed I was insignificant and unattractive. I was also told many times that I was mean. I tried to believe that, but my thoughts immediately rejected it whenever it was said to me. I would think, *"I'm not mean. I just don't like anybody messing with me."* That *"messing"* is another book in itself. Anyway, I had a mindset, and I lived in that life every day. I was a product of my environment.

Even though I was blood born into my family, every day of my youth, I believed with all my heart that I was adopted. I used to tell my "friend" that I believed I was adopted, and one day I would find out that I belonged to another set of parents. I totally believed that because I was so different. I believed that was why I was misdiagnosed in their eyes.

Growing up, I heard many voices speaking and deciding who I was. I heard family members say, *"Tonja Lyn is so mean," "You're silly," "Tonja is sneaky," "You're stupid,"* and many more things were spoken. But none of them were true; that was not who I was. They misdiagnosed me, but it was not their fault. They did not know who I truly was, and I did not know who I was either. I did know that I was not those things *they* said I was.

I cannot recall play by play or minute by minute the accounts of my childhood. I only have one memory of anything before ten years old, and I barely remember the few preteen and teen years. I remember what I call milestones. I remember snapshots of experiences or occurrences that happened at one time or another. I am able to remember them because these snapshots were defining moments; they were the moments that shaped my mindset. As I reflect while writing this book, I can recall moments that helped me to understand questions I had unanswered for years in my mind. For example, I often questioned why my mother did not know how much I loved her.

As a child, my mother and I had a very loving relationship. I adored my mother; however, somewhere along the way of life, my mother lost sight of the love I had for her, maybe because I stopped saying it. I have a snapshot memory of being a child. I am pretty sure it was before I was ten. We lived on Richland Street in Columbia, South Carolina. I slept at the bottom of a set of bunk beds. Every single morning, I remember rolling over, getting out of bed, and heading straight for the kitchen. Without fail, my mother would be at the stove stirring grits. I would walk over to her and say, *"I love you, momma,"* and each time she would respond by saying, *"I love you too, baby."* I would then turn around and leave to get ready for school or watch cartoons. I also have a snapshot memory of years later, as a teen, when my mother and I were not in agreement about something. She turned to me and asked, *"Why do you hate me so much?"* I was stunned! In that flash of a moment, it felt like ninety-nine thoughts went through my head. I thought, *"Where in the world did she get that from? Hate her? I don't hate her! She's actually a really good mother. She's just not good at listening to what I have to say. She takes a little bit of what she heard and runs off with her interpretation of what she thinks the rest is about. What makes her think I don't love her? I use to tell her that every day when I was little. How did we get here? How did it come to this?"* Thought after thought came pouring out of my head, but the only words I could muster up were, "I don't hate you." That was it. Should I have countered with, *"I do love you, Momma. I love you very much?"* Would that have been the turning point back to those moments in the kitchen? Would that have uprooted whatever I had done or did not do over the years that sent my mother the message that I did not love her? I do not know because all I said was, "I don't hate you." Then, I went back into my thoughts while she went on with, *"Yes, you do. You wouldn't treat me like you do if you did."* I do not remember anything else she said. I shut down.

We were not an affectionate family. I do not remember getting hugs or hearing "*I love you*" coming from any member of my family toward me or even toward each other. I do not even remember the spouses saying, "*I love you*" to each other. So, knowing I was loved did not get imparted anymore after those kitchen visits in my memory.

Some snapshots were moments that validate that my *"Daddy"* was protecting me all of my life until the day we would meet in person. Some snapshot moments confirmed that I was not wrong about the belief that I was more than what I was living, hearing, and believing.

I had become a product of my environment and experiences. The voices of those around me defined who I was, *"I was mean,"* *"I was sneaky,"* *"I was hateful,"* *"I was antisocial,"* *"I was ..."* The list goes on and on, but the day I met my *"Daddy"* was the day He began to introduce me to a new me. He began the process of manifesting the person I was to be at the moment of my conception. He would fashion, mold, and shape me into the person He created me to be: the real me.

GET OUT YOUR JOURNALS:

Recall a milestone moment in your childhood. Is there a defining snapshot that comes to mind?

Chapter 5
First Things First

I was so excited and in awe that the sovereign God of heaven had made Himself real to me, and now I had the opportunity and the right to call Him Father. I did not know that as our relationship developed, I would be so in love with Him that He would affectionately be known to me as *"Daddy."*

After meeting *"Daddy,"* the first thing I had to do was learn how to trust Him with *"the process;"* a *"process"* that I was very unfamiliar with, possibly because I had never been exposed to anyone who had endured His *"processing."* If I had been exposed to such persons, they never took the time to enlighten me on what that *"process"* entailed. As a matter of fact, the night I met my *"Daddy,"* I had no clue there was such a thing as a *"process."* I learned that along the way from the teachings I received within the ministry I was planted and the teachings I received personally from *"Daddy."* Ultimately, all the teachings came from *"Daddy."*

In my first lesson, *"Daddy"* had to empty me. He had to remove all the things that were not like Him. *"Daddy"* had to dispel all the "junk" my foster parent and the devil had put there. Remember in John 8:44 (NLT) when Jesus told the people, *"For you are the*

children of your father the devil, and you love to do the evil things he does. He was a murderer from the beginning. He has always hated the truth, because there is no truth in him. When he lies, it is consistent with his character; for he is a liar and the father of lies."
Well, the devil was my foster parent; I was of that "father," the devil. I lied to get out and to stay out of trouble. I murdered someone's reputation when I gossiped about them. I murdered someone's character when I lied about them knowingly because I wanted revenge or unknowingly because I was repeating something someone told me without any evidence that the information was true. Either way, those repeated actions were of the devil and had no part of who God was. Those actions and decisions were the actions of my foster father, the devil, not the actions of my true Father, the sovereign God of heaven.

Before *"Daddy"* could begin the process of emptying me, I had to first learn how to trust Him or I would never endure to the end and become a mature saint. I remember my first set of lessons on trust. Those were the most difficult ones for me because I was very independent. I had developed a mindset that, by all means, I was going to take care of myself. My mind was set on not allowing myself to become dependent on anyone. When you are dependent on someone else, that person has control over you; you must dance to their music, and if you refuse, they could manipulate you because they have what you need. I was not going to let that happen in my life anymore. If I needed something, I was going to work to get it myself. Even if I had to work two or three jobs, I would never allow myself to depend on some man to give me what I needed. I was determined that being an independent woman was non-negotiable. That mindset strengthened as the years went by due to spoiled relationships. Therefore, when "*Daddy*" began to work with me on trust, He certainly had some amount of work cut out for Him.

Those lessons on trust were the most important ones for me. If I did not trust "*Daddy*," where else was there to go from that point? During my lessons on trust, "*Daddy*" would maneuver situations that were out of my control to handle on my own, so I could see that He would come through for me. He wanted and needed me to see that He could and would always take care of me. I just needed to know what it looked like. So, He would allow a circumstance or problem to arise, and then He would lay it on someone's heart to bless me with the solution to my dilemma. In my baby stage, the solutions were obvious and quick, for example, when I needed a certain amount of money to afford my baby's daycare fee for a week. If I was unable to take my baby to the daycare, I would not be able to work so I could pay to keep the roof over our heads or buy groceries and other necessities that my paycheck covered. Although I was very distracted by my pending dilemma, I went to church that Sunday. On my way out of the building, a lady came to me and said, "Sis Tonja, the Lord led me to give this to you." While I was looking at her, she squeezed some folded papers into my hand. I then looked down to see that the papers were dollar bills. I felt it was rude to count the money right there on the spot in her presence, so I hugged her, thanked her for her gift, and continued on out of the building. When I got in the car, I took the bills out of my pocket. Taking them in both hands, I spread them apart to discover that the paper dollars counted to the exact amount I needed for the daycare. I cried all the way home from church, knowing I had the means to go to work and earn money to pay the rent and put food on the table once again. But, most of all, I had an overwhelming, concrete knowledge that God had provided the solution to my dilemma through that dear sister who knew nothing about it. *"Daddy"* was making Himself real in my life.

Another such incident was a time when the electricity was disconnected due to non-payment. In spite of my overwhelming distraction with my current circumstances, I went to church. It was a Saturday service at the main church on what was then Carondelet Street in New Orleans. As always, I enjoyed the service immensely. At the end, I got up and went to the restroom. Upon my return, I heard "The Prophet" say, "She better hurry back. She's about to miss this blessing." I thought he was speaking of someone in the service at the time. When I entered the sanctuary, he called me down to him. He then motioned for a gentleman to come stand next to me with an offering basket. I did not know what was going on. I thought "Prophet" was going to ask me to give a special offering or something. I would have wanted to be obedient, but I was standing there thinking, *"I don't even have lights on at my house; I don't know what in the world I'm going to put in that basket."* At that moment, "Prophet" said, "I want everyone that will be obedient to my voice to come and put something in this basket for her. The Lord told me to take up a special offering for her. Now come." The people started getting up out of their seats from all over the sanctuary. When I realized what was happening, I was overwhelmed with gratefulness. I could not stop crying. After the people stopped coming, "Prophet" told the man to count the money, put it in an envelope and give it to me. I went straight to the electric company. So, you see, in the beginning of my walk with God, He built my trust through interactions that showed me it was obviously His hand that came through on my behalf because no one who was involved with the solution had knowledge of my dilemma.

As I began to grow in His Word, the lessons on trust stopped coming so quickly and obviously. I have come a long way from those quick and obvious solutions. As I matured, my trust in Him required me to have a bit more faith at every season in the various lessons. He is still giving me trust lessons. I do not think those lessons will ever stop while we are here on earth. As we mature from milk to meat, our lessons require our faith to *"work"* towards the solutions to our dilemmas. He has already provided the way to the solution. However, our faith and obedience is the key that unlocks the window that pours out that solution. Sometimes I miss those quick and obvious solutions. They were easier but I would take nothing away from the work it requires for my faith to endure in order for me to get manifested answers to my prayers. The working of your faith makes for good testimonies. Good testimonies increase faith and empower others to overcome. Sometimes in the working of this faith, I get weary in well-doing, frustrated, sick and tired of waiting, nervous in the silence, impatient, tears, among other negative feelings. But, at the manifestation of that answered prayer is a deeper trust in *"Daddy"* that He will never leave me nor forsake me, just like He promised.

GET OUT YOUR JOURNALS:

Journal your first trust lesson with God. Write about:

a) the area you trust God the most.
b) the area you trust God the least.
c) the greatest trial you have faced so far in your walk with God.

Chapter 6
In Daddy's Presence

There was something about "Daddy's" presence. Every time I was in His presence, it was like nothing I had ever experienced before. You would think with all His responsibilities that He would not have a lot of time for me. But the more time I spent with Him, the more time He wanted to spend with me. Initially, the time I made for Him was exactly that: it was time I *made* for Him. It felt like a chore, a duty of some sort, but as time went on, the more time I spent with Him, the more time I wanted to spend with Him. I realized my mindset about my desire to be "*saved*" had changed.

Previously, I wanted to be "saved" because the thought of burning in hell forever scared that same "hell" out of me. I did not want any part of hell. I felt like, *"I just got to be save. I can't stand that thought of burning forever with no chance of getting out or getting relief."* So, for me, salvation was not an option. I believed hell was real, so I needed to find out how to secure my place in heaven. To do that meant accepting salvation and getting saved. To do that was believing the gospel of the Bible. To do that, I had to get to know the God that put it all in place for me. I say it like that because I had to take it personally. I could not count on anybody else to mess this up for me. What if I believed the wrong things based on someone else's faith, then found myself in hell after all? I could not take that chance. I had to see for myself which religion was truth for me. That inquiry ignited within me a strong desire to have a personal relationship with *"The God"* I had been hearing about for so many years. I did have sense enough to know that if you are going to be in a relationship with someone, spending time with them is vital to that union's progress. So, I knew I had to spend time with *"Daddy."* Therefore, as I said before, initially, I spent time with *"Daddy"* out of obligation and to feed my selfish desire to NOT spend eternity in a burning furnace, falling with no end in sight—and speaking of "sight," if there was a bottom, you would not see it anyway. Mathew 22:13 says hell is a place of outer darkness. I did not want to know what that looked like. Therefore, I had to get to know *"The God."*

Hanging out with *"Daddy"* began to change my reasons for wanting to be saved. I was no longer seeking the "saved" life to escape hell. I was securing the "saved" life because I did not want to be separate from the feeling I got when I was with *"Daddy."* Being with *"Daddy"* not only felt good, but it was doing something to me and doing something in me. I did not want it to stop. It was good for me. I was loving who I was becoming. When I was with Him, He would put a mirror in front of me and show me who I was in Him. It was difficult to believe Him at first, but I had to believe Him; He cannot lie. That mirror was powerful. It was in my reach all along. Sometimes that mirror was right in the palm of my hands, but I never positioned it correctly in order to view myself the way *"Daddy"* designed me to see myself. That mirror was the Bible. In that Bible, *"Daddy"* was showing me who I was to Him. He was showing me what I was to Him. He was showing me the plans He had for me, even from the day of my birth, even from the day of my conception. All of this was hidden from me in plain view by my "stepfather," the devil. Through the devil's tactics and strategies, it was his goal to keep this knowledge and truth from me so I would die in my sins and never fulfill the powerful work my true *"Daddy"* had for me to complete. . . the devil wins. The devil's desire is for me to never know who my true Father is because if I did, the devil lost. The devil does not like to lose. You would think he would be used to it by now, always going up against *"Daddy,"* but *"Daddy"* NEVER loses. I see the devil's tactics this way: he knows he is going to lose the ultimate battle against *"Daddy,"* so he has decided and is determine to take as many casualties as he possibly can with him. I have concluded and am determined to NOT be one of the devil's casualties. I desire for you to come to that conclusion as well.

I was falling in love with the presence of *"Daddy."* It was an awesome feeling. In His presence, the bad stuff was going away, and the good stuff was coming in. In His presence, I was being taught, renewed, restored, strengthened, and empowered. In His presence, I was being made aware that I have a purpose. For the first time, I was hearing and seeing that I had value. I was not an accident. I was fearfully and wonderfully made:

> **Psalms 139:14** - *I will praise thee; for I am fearfully and wonderfully made: marvelous are thy works; and that my soul knoweth right well. (KJV).*

For the first time, I came into the knowledge that I am "Daddy's" masterpiece, and He had planned for me to do good things for Him and His kingdom a long time ago:

> **Ephesians 2:10** – *For we are God's masterpiece. He has created us anew in Christ Jesus, so we can do the good things he planned for us long ago. (NLT).*

In His presence, I was coming into the knowledge that there was nothing I could not accomplish in Him because He would PERSONALLY see to it that I succeeded:

> **Deuteronomy 31:6** - *So be strong and courageous! Do not be afraid and do not panic before them. For the Lord your God will **personally** go ahead of you. He will neither fail you nor abandon you. (NLT).*

In His presence, I was enjoying Him so much. In His presence, He was taking such delight in me being there:

> **Proverbs 8:30** - *I was the architect at his side. I was his constant delight, rejoicing always in his presence. (NLT).*

Knowing He delighted in me made me feel special and wanted. I was falling in love with *"Daddy's"* presence because in *"Daddy's"* presence, He was mine, and I was His. In His presence, I was *Daddy's Little Girl*.

Okay, so now that I was there, what next? Why was that such a big deal for me? Let us explore what that means for me, and if you find some part of its importance to me to be of equal importance to you, it was worth my time to write this book.

GET OUT YOUR JOURNALS:

Journal on your understanding of what it means to "be saved." Does it still mean that to you?

a) What does your time with God look like?
b) Where do you spend time with God?
c) How long is your time spent with God in that place?
d) What do you do when you are there spending time with God?
e) Journal about a noticeable change that has taken place in your life since you have been spending time with God.

Chapter 7
Why Did I Want To Be A Daddy's Little Girl

*I*n that room that day, in that most vulnerable time in my moment of moments, why did I ask to be a *"Daddy's Little Girl?"* Why was that position of "Daddy's Little Girl" so important to me that I desired it for so many years, even into my adulthood? Why not ask an all-powerful, sovereign God to make me a warrior, so no one would be able to overpower me, and I would always be safe? Why not ask Him to make me a healer so I could go around and make people feel better? Why did I not ask to be a mighty successful intercessor so I could pray for the things that grieved my God and open the gateways for Him to intervene in those matters? But no, I asked to be a "Daddy's Little Girl." What was that all about? To know that answer, you have to know a few more details about my story.

Remember in chapter 4, *"Becoming Who I Was,"* when I told my mother every morning that I loved her and then years later she believed I hated her? I wondered what had happened. Well, a lot of "life" happened. During those years, I experienced encounters and interactions that were not Godly. Those encounters and interactions should never have been introduced or presented to a little girl by a grown man. It was abuse, but I did not know it was abuse while it was happening. I just knew I did not like it, and I did not want it to happen anymore. The experience was foreign to me, so I did not know it was wrong. I just knew something did not feel right about it. I did not know I was supposed to tell someone about it, and because I did not do that, it went on far too long.

As it continued to happen over a period of time, I became someone I was not born to be. I began to act in a way I believed would protect me from any other abuser with a notion to do the same. I became skilled at my defense mechanisms; they became my walls of protection. I had to have these walls as they kept the enemy from getting too close. If no one could get close, then no one could hurt me again. Since I could not always tell who the bad guys were, I wanted to keep everybody out. I became skilled at my defense methods. My walls were vital to my existence and safety.

One tactic I used looked like a wrinkled brow of anger. I can remember in high school, I was often asked if I was mad about something or who made me mad. My response to them was always "No" or "Nobody." It was the truth. No one had made me mad at that moment. If my schoolmates thought I was mad, that told me my particular method of defense that day was effective. People usually create distance between themself and a mad person. That was what I wanted: distance. The wrinkled brow was a keeper.

I remember my grandmother, Wilhelmina, telling me, *"Tonja, stop wrinkling up your face like that. It's going to become permanent."* Her words were not enough to stop me from doing it, but her words came to pass. When I look at pictures of myself, no matter how broad the smile is on my face, my forehead looks like I am wrinkling it on purpose. The wrinkled forehead had become permanent, just like my grandmother said. I have to live with that. I chose to continue that defense strategy throughout the years, and it was effective.

Another tactic I used was staying out of the way. When family events came about, whether my mom took me to those events or the events came to us, I disappeared as much as possible. Too many people meant trouble. Remember, in that same chapter, I told you how I was misdiagnosed? Well, my methods were the reason why. My methods kept people at a distance. That distance was a part of my safety maneuver. That distance also made me seem "*antisocial*" to others, just like that wrinkled brow made me look "*mean*." I stayed out of people's way so I would not become a target, and that made me look "*sneaky*," so I was misdiagnosed; I was none of those things. Those things were just my methods to protect myself from abusers.

Maybe if the abuse had never happened, I would have asked to be a warrior in my daughter's room that day. If the abuse had never happened, maybe I would have had a passionate heart to intercede for humanity. Who knows? What I do know is that my experiences were my reality, and my reality shaped the Tonja I was before "*Daddy*" brought me truth. My walls were perceived as "*walls of anger*," "*walls of mean*," "*walls of sneaky*," "*walls of antisocial*," "*walls of hateful*," among others. No matter how many times I would hear these labels spoken on, over, or about me, I knew they were not true. I may not have known what or who I really was, but I knew I was not any of those things.

Sometimes it hurts to hear those words come from someone I really loved. The pain was in the fact that the person could not see the real me. That family member who was supposed to love me could not perceive the real me. They could only perceive my façade, my walls. That was the source of my anger. I wanted someone to see me, the real me. I wanted somebody to see the me that was caring, and compassionate. I wanted them to see the me that would cry at the sight of someone suffering. Mean people do not do that; mean people do not care, but I cared a lot. Therefore, year after year, I was misdiagnosed, and year after year, I kept the walls up. This led me to live an isolated life. I needed those walls; they were necessary; they had to be there. To tear them down was risky, and that was a risk I was not willing to take. Therefore, I endured the misdiagnosis. I endured the mistreatment from others because of who they thought I was. I endured the offensive words made by some because of their misinterpretation of Tonja. I endured it all. Notice, I did not say I accepted it. It hurt, but I did not let them know that. There was a deodorant commercial years ago that I took on as my motto. The slogan was *"Never Let 'Em See You Sweat."* I had to stand tough. I endured it, but I never accepted those opinions of me; I never embraced them. But I must admit, I lived the façade for so long that at times I wondered if I had actually become the person they said I was. That only lasted briefly. I may not have known who I really was, but I knew who I was not.

GET OUT YOUR JOURNALS:

Journal a time you had a "misdiagnosis." How did you handle it? What were your thoughts afterward?

Journal your desire to be a "Daddy's Little Girl."

Chapter 8
Self-Proclaimed Or Authentic

My interpretation of a *"Daddy's Little Girl"* came from the television shows and movies I watched, but you cannot always believe what you see on television, right? Well, I concluded that the television shows had to base their representation of that *"Daddy's Little Girl"* on someone's truth. Now that I was a self-proclaimed *"Daddy's Little Girl,"* I sought to validate if I was authentic. Could I really proclaim myself as *"Daddy's Little Girl?"* Did I have all the qualities and the mindset of a *"Daddy's Little Girl?"* Could I or would I base my claim on one ambiguous resource, such as a television show or shows. I needed something else to compare my authenticity to. I needed to know I was the real deal.

The best way to get factual evidence was to pull on an original source. In Social Studies, it is called a primary resource. This means the source was involved in the matter or was there as an eyewitness to the accounts. In Science, you test the prediction by testing the theory two or three times before you can declare it proven. The best way to validate the testing of the theory is to test with more than one variable (*I think*). Science was never my best subject in school.

43

I made it out of Science classes, but it was not because I mastered the material; it was definitely by the grace of God.

In case I did not quite get that illustration correct, let me present this one. When you are in court, the best witness is someone who was there on the scene: an eyewitness. It would be awesome to have more than one eyewitness to add more credibility to the proven theory. If you cannot get the original document or an eyewitness, you must get as close as possible to the original or authentic thing. I needed to prove I was the real deal; therefore, I needed my sources to be the real deals. I decided to prove my validity by interviewing several true original *"Daddy's Little Girls."*

I had worked with my colleagues for a year, so I knew them well enough to analyze and determine the ones who were a *"Daddy's Little Girl"* and the ones who were not. Based on what I had concluded about *"Daddy's Little Girls,"* they carried themselves a certain way and exhibited a certain amount of confidence. When they talked about their family moments, they called the name *"Daddy"* with a deep sense of endearment, almost to the point of annoyance. Based on these criteria, I had my targeted co-workers in mind. Without informing them of the interview or the purpose of the interview, I asked them the following four questions:

    a. Who is a "Daddy's Little Girl?"
    b. What are the benefits of being a "Daddy's Little Girl?"
    c. How do you feel in "Daddy's" presence?
    d. How do you feel outside of "Daddy's" presence?

Courtney was the first of the "*Daddy's Little Girl*s" I interviewed. Even as Courtney answered her four questions, she radiated with excitement and that annoying endearment as she discussed and elaborated about her "*Daddy.*" Well, in Courtney's case, it was "Daddy(s)" with the "s." Courtney was fortunate enough to be the "*Daddy's Little Girl*" of a biological father as well as a step-father. Now that is what I call a primary resource self-confirmed. Also, as Courtney gave her responses, I was about to burst on the inside. At each response, I was shouting within myself, "*THAT'S EXACTLY HOW I FEEL ABOUT MY DADDY!*" So far, Courtney had confirmed my validity for me, but I could not stop there. I had to validate with more than one subject. I left Courtney, determined to find the opportune time and place to pull the others aside for the four-question interview. I could not wait to hear what all the other ladies had to say. At the conclusion of my research, sixty-seven percent (67%) of the targets had nearly identical answers. The only difference was the varying in the sentence structure of their responses.

Therefore, Courtney's responses, and the fact that her answers were self-confirmed in her position of being a "Daddy's Little Girl" to a step-father and a blood father, became my primary source for the comparison I would make to validate my status as a bona fide, authentic "*Daddy's Little Girl.*" I will reveal and address each interview response in its own chapter so as not to overwhelm or confuse any of the qualities in the comparison and validation of my status. At the end, I will, and I am sure you will as well, see that without the shadow of a doubt, I can emphatically declare to the world that I am a "*Daddy's Little Girl.*"

Maybe you grew up without a father or a father figure, as so many in this country have. If being a *"Daddy's Little Girl"* has been your desire as well, you will be excited to know that it is not impossible just because you grew up without a father. It is not too late because you are a grown woman now. You will discover that the opportunity still awaits you to become a *"Daddy's Little Girl."*

Read on.

GET OUT YOUR JOURNALS:

Journal your definition and/or characteristics of a "Daddy's Little Girl."

Chapter 9
What Is A Daddy's Little Girl

As said in the previous chapter, my interpretation, revelation, and conclusion of what classified a *"Daddy's Little Girl"* was confirmed in my research. I could now confidently declare that I was a member of this elite group of women. I can now go out and buy my t-shirt to proudly display *"Daddy's Little Girl"* without feeling like an imposter.

We will begin with the first question, "Who is a Daddy's Little Girl"? I could have begun with any one of the candidates within the study to make my comparisons but, for the sake of time and space, I will grab any one of the other participants and Courtney.

Participant 1: "Someone who follows him around. They do what they do. They want to be with him all the time."

Courtney: "I know that over everything or through any situation, my daddy is going to come through for me, whether it is *'I want…'*, *'I need…'*, or *'This happened…'*, my daddy is going to always be there. I can go to him and ask, *'Daddy, can I get these shoes?'* and he says *'No, you can't get those shoes, they cost $200,'* but then I end up with the shoes; or *'Daddy, this happened and this hurt my* *feelings and I need you. What do you think?'* That, to me, is a Daddy's Little Girl."

Let us explore these two answers as compared to how I view my heavenly Father.

1. "...**I want to follow Him around all the time**." I want to follow my "Daddy" around all the time. How do I follow a sovereign God around all the time? You follow Him by following His Son, Jesus. Luke 9:35 (NLT) tells us what the sovereign God said when the transfiguration took place: *"Then a voice from the cloud said, 'This is my Son, my Chosen One. Listen to him.'"* So, I follow my Daddy around by following Jesus.

   John, speaking of Jesus in Chapter 3 verse 34 (NLT) says, *"For he is sent by God, He speaks God's words, for God gives him the Spirit without limit."* Jesus commands us to follow Him as well. He even gave us the benefits of that obedience in Matthew 19:27 (NLT) after Peter asked a seemingly offensive question. Peter said, *"We've given up everything for you."* Then he asked, *"What will we get?"* I thought that was a fair enough question. I do not know if I would have been bold enough to ask it, but I sure would have wondered about that from time to time. Jesus did not take offense. He gave Peter the answer he sought. Jesus said in Matthew 19:29 – (NLT), *"And everyone who has given up houses or brothers or sisters or father or mother or children or property, for my sake, will receive a hundred times as much in return and will inherit eternal life."* That is a pretty good deal. So, how do I follow my "Daddy" around? I do it by following His Son, Jesus, and not just one time, but continuously. **Colossians 2:6** states, *"And now, just as you accepted Christ Jesus as your Lord, you must continue to follow him." (NLT)*. I strive every day to walk in the principles, practices, and commands of Jesus. This obedience keeps me close to my "Daddy."

2. **"…She knows that over everything or through any situation, her daddy is going to come through for her."** My *"Daddy"* gives all kinds of promises to this quality of a "Daddy's Little Girl." I know that through everything and through every situation, my daddy is going to come through for me. My favorite promise is Isaiah 43:2 (NLT), *"When you go through deep waters, I will be with you. When you go through rivers of **difficulty**, you will not drown. When you walk through the fire of **oppression**, you will not be burned up; the flames will not consume you."* (emphasis mine). Every girl faces difficulty at some point in her life. I have faced many difficulties, but my *"Daddy"* has not allowed those difficulties to overwhelm me. Many women have been the victim of *"oppression,"* which is the state of being subject to unjust treatment or control. If you take a minute and reflect, you may be able to think of several interactions of relationships where you have been the subject to oppression. It could have been a boyfriend or husband, a boss, a best friend, or so you thought. Whatever the level of that relationship, you were affected by oppression. I experienced oppression just last year on my job, but my *"Daddy"* did not allow me to be burnt in that situation. The flames of their bullying tactics did not consume me. I was

still able to do my job and overcome the desire to seek revenge.

3. **"…Daddy, this happened, and this hurt my feelings, and I need you. What do you think?"** I hear the "Daddy's Little Girl" seeking comfort from her daddy. I have lost count of the times I have needed comforting from and for one matter and then another. Before "Daddy" truly came into my life, no resource or person I sought could apply the complete balm I needed to be comforted. Even though, at times, it seemed successful, it proved only temporary. When *"Daddy"* came into my life, and I began to go to *"Daddy"* about my hurt and with my questions, the comfort He gave me was permanent and eternal. The best part for me was, once I overcame and was comforted through my *"Daddy's"* maneuvers, the healing of each matter could be used as ministry. I was able to help someone who was facing the same dilemmas. That part made me feel empowered and needed, like I had a purpose in life.

> **2 Corinthians 1:4** (NLT) – *He comforts us in all our troubles so that we can comfort others. When they are troubled, we will be able to give them the same comfort God has given us.*

Many times, my *"Daddy"* gives His promises to be a comfort to me.

> **Psalm 119:50** – *Your promise revives me; it comforts me in all my troubles.* (NLT).

Isaiah 12:1 – *In that day you will sing; "I will praise you, O Lord! You were angry with me, but not anymore. Now, you comfort me."* (NLT).

Psalm 86:17 – *Send me a sign of your favor. Then those who hate me will be put to shame, for you O Lord, help and comfort me.* (NLT).

Psalm 94:19 – *When doubts filled my mind, your comfort gave me renewed hope and cheer.* (NLT).

Psalm 23:4b - *...Your rod and your staff protect and comfort me.* (NLT).

Psalm 59:10 - *In his unfailing love, my God will stand with me. He will let me look down in triumph on all my enemies.* (NLT)

When Jesus was talking to the disciples in **John 14,** He did not just promise comfort, He promised a Comforter: a Person who is totally dedicated to comforting you in your time of need. Jesus said in **verse 26** (KJV)**,** *"But the Comforter, which is the Holy Ghost, whom the Father will send in my name, he shall teach you all things, and bring all things to your remembrance, whatsoever I have said unto you."* When we need answers, the Comforter will teach us. When we forget the promises and love of God, the Comforter will bring all those promises back to our remembrance.

I am living in a perpetual mindset of knowing without the shadow of a doubt that my *"Daddy"* loves me, His little princess.

GET OUT YOUR JOURNALS:

How often do you want to be with God? Do you only think about it on Sundays? Do you only think about it when you are in trouble and need help? Do you make time daily to be alone with God?

    a) Journal a situation where the only person you could give credit to for bringing you out is God.

Chapter 10
The Benefits Of Being A Daddy's Little Girl

In the second question, all but one participant had the same answer. That majority answered, *"The benefit of being a 'Daddy's Little Girl' is to know how a man is supposed to treat you."* So, let us compare that response with that of my mindset towards my *"Daddy."*

Survey Response: "...**The biggest benefit is to know how a man is supposed to treat you**." This answer was parallel to my mindset about my *"Daddy."* God is relational; He is very family-oriented, so much so that He made a woman to keep man company and to help him throughout all the ages of the earth. No matter what decisions he made, the woman was to *"help"* him fulfill the will of God on the earth. One way she was to do this was to partner with the man to procreate. ***Genesis 1:27b-28a*** (NLT) states *"...male and female he created them. Then God blessed them and said, 'Be fruitful and multiply. Fill the earth and govern it."* I brought that up to point out that a woman and a man are going to come together. It is the way God designed it from the beginning.

If you are still not convinced, let us go over to the New Testament. In ***1 Corinthians 11:9*** (NLT), it says, *"And man was not made for* *woman, but woman was made for man.*" A man cannot bring forth human fruit of his own kind within the make-up of what a male is; he needs a woman to "*help*" with that. One more, ***I Corinthians 11:11*** (NLT) says, "*But among the Lord's people, women are not independent of men, and men are not independent of women.*" This means the man needs the woman and the woman needs the man. So, when you and your man come together, it is ordained and sanctioned by God, but you must understand and KNOW that the man you are coming together with is of God. How will you know that? There is a certain way that a man is supposed to treat you. He is supposed to treat you according to the standards of God. What are the standards of God? The standards are laid out in God's Word.

1. **He should love you like Christ loved his bride. (The Church) – Ephesians 5:25** (NLT) - *"For husbands, this means love your wives, just as Christ loved the church. He gave up his life for her."*

Your man must love you like Christ loved and still loves His church. Christ died for His bride. Should your man be willing to jump in front of a bullet for you? Yes, but not just that. In many cases of arguments between a couple, it goes on too far for too long and ends up in divorce court because at least one of the two is not willing to give up their right to be right. When there is a disagreement or a challenging situation that comes up in your relationship, your man should be willing to die to himself for you. This means he should be willing to give up his male ego and pride to bring you back in right standing with him. That is what Christ would do.

2. **He should be a man you can totally submit to in everything.**

Ephesians 5:24 (NLT) - *"As the church submits to Christ, so you wives should submit to your husbands in everything."*

If there is an area you are not willing to submit to with *"that"* man, you are not ready to be his wife. Submission does not mean being a puppet so you follow and do everything he says. The word *"submit"* is a verb that has two meanings. One is to *"accept or yield to the authority of another person."* The other is *"present to a person or body for consideration or judgment."* Both definitions work hand in hand within your relationship. Wife, when your husband is facing or making a decision on a situation that you may not feel at peace about, you should be able to present your concerns to your authority (*your husband*) for consideration. You do know your husband is the authority, right? The man is the head of the woman (See *I Corinthians 11:3*). Well, you should be able to talk to him about your concerns, and those concerns should be considered in or before his final decision.

3. **He should be willing to be the head of his house. Ephesians 4:15** (NLT) – *"Instead, we will speak the truth in love, growing in every way more and more like Christ, who is the head of his body, the church."*

Some men are content allowing the woman to lead. Some find safety in that because they have someone to blame if things go wrong. Some find safety in that because they have been "over-mothered," if you know what I mean. Some find safety in that because they are just plain trifling. A real man, a man who loves Jesus and truly loves you, will be willing to take the lead and lead his family. When he takes on a wife, something awakens in him, and he fully accepts this responsibility and all the dings, bells, whistles, and arrows that come with that responsibility. He will always tell you the truth, but not in a mean or demeaning manner. His truth will always be from a heart of love. He will always be willing to grow more and more like Christ by going to church, studying the Word of God, and praying for and with his family.

4. **He must love the Lord. 1 Corinthians 16:22** (NLT) - *"If anyone does not love the Lord, that person is cursed. Our Lord, come!"*

ENOUGH SAID. If your man does not love the Lord, your relationship is destined for problems that God did not intend for you to endure.

All the ways your man is supposed to love you, my *"Daddy"* loves me that way. So, just like Courtney, my huge benefit of being a *"Daddy's Little Girl"* is to know how a man is supposed to treat me because my *"Daddy"* lays it out in His Word.

GET OUT YOUR JOURNALS:

Journal your hesitations about totally submitting to a man in EVERY situation.

a) Do you want to run the house?
b) Does the man in your life share your love for God?
c) Does the man in your life support your love for God?

Chapter 11
A Daddy's Little Girl In Her Daddy's Presence

*I*n this third question, again all but one participant had the same answer. That majority answered, *"The benefit of being in daddy's presence is that I feel safe."*

This answer was parallel to my mindset towards my *"Daddy."* My *"Daddy"* has written a book. Although it has been around for centuries, I never knew I had a book written just for me by my very own Father. I heard about *"This Book"*; I heard people speak about and from *"This Book"*; I even heard songs about the contents of *"This Book"*; but I never knew *"This Book"* was specifically and personally written for me.

When I discovered who I truly was and began to spend time with my *"Daddy,"* I found out He wrote *"This Book"* with the hope that one day I would read it and know the love and plans He has for me. It saddened Him to see me living a defeated life and lifestyle when He had an abundant life mapped out for me. *"Daddy"* and I began to spend time together reading through *"The Book."* It told me who I was, but, most importantly, it told me who HE was. Each time I read "*This Book*," I saw the personality of my "*Daddy*." I began to understand life as He meant it for me. I began to know His ways, like what makes Him angry and what brings Him joy. "*The Book*" helped me to know His will for me;

1. **Eternal life** - **1 Peter 4:6** (NLT) - *"That is why the Good News was preached to those who are now dead—so although they were destined to die like all people, they now live forever with God in the Spirit."*

2. **Good success** - **Deuteronomy 30:9** (NLT) – *"The Lord your God will **then** make you successful in **everything** you do. He will give you many children and numerous livestock, and he will cause your fields to produce abundant harvests, for the Lord will again delight in being good to you as he was to your ancestors."* (emphasis mine).

(Disclaimer: There is a prerequisite to this promise. Make sure you find out what the prerequisite is.)

3. **Life more abundantly** - **John 10:10** (NLT) - *"The thief's purpose is to steal and kill and destroy. My purpose is to give them a rich and satisfying life."*

4. **Holy living** - **Leviticus 20:26** (NLT) - **"*You* must be holy because I, the Lord, am holy. I have set you apart from all other people to be my very own."** (emphasis mine). **1 Thessalonians 4:7** (NLT) - **"***God has called us to live holy lives, not impure lives.***"**

So, as you can see, eternal life, good success, life more abundantly, and holy living are benefits of being *"Daddy's"* child.

Let us get back to the third survey question to the "Daddy's Little Girls": *"What is a benefit of being in daddy's presence?"* The overwhelming response was: *"The benefit of being in daddy's presence is that I feel safe."* My safety was also in *"This Book"* my *"Daddy"* wrote to me.

> 1. **Psalm 4:8** (NLT) - *"In peace I will lie down and sleep, for you alone, O Lord, will keep me safe."*

I read this quote somewhere: "Why should I stay up and worry? God is up anyway." If those are not the exact words, I have captured the gist of it. The bottom line is, my "Daddy" will keep me safe, period! So, I can sleep well at nights. Staying up worrying about *"it"* is not going to change *"it."* So I go to bed, and I sleep because I KNOW my *"Daddy"* is going to cause all things to work out for my good, and because of that, I feel safe.

> 2. **Proverbs 18:10** (NLT) - *"The name of the Lord is a strong fortress; the godly run to him and are safe."*

Whenever life gets overwhelming for me, I call the name of my *"Daddy."* I find time to withdraw from responsibilities so that I can spend time with *"Daddy"* alone. When I am in that alone time with Him, I find comfort, peace, and strength. After this personal time with *"Daddy,"* I can come out and face the world once more. I can do this because I know the next time the world gets overwhelming for me, I can call on my *"Daddy,"* and He is always there. He will always have time for me. He will always be waiting for me to come to Him and bring all my troubles. He longs for my company. He loves to pour out His love on me.

In my "*Daddy's*" presence, I feel safe.

GET OUT YOUR JOURNALS:

Journal about who God is to you.

- a) What is God's will for you?
- b) What threatens your safety?
- c) What makes you feel safe?

Chapter 12
A Daddy's Little Girl Out Of Her Daddy's Presence

In this fourth and final survey question, the participants answered, *"When I'm out of daddy's presence, I'm always trying to get back there."*

That answer hit home in a very personal way for me. I feel so safe when I am with *"Daddy,"* I NEVER want to leave His presence. Safety is very important to me. It may be a woman thing or a Tonja thing, but the biggest comfort I have in all of the relationships I value is that I feel safe in them. When I am with these valued persons, I know I am getting the real them. I know I can be the real me without the result or consequence of a false diagnosis. I am so free around these people of value, and that freedom with them brings me comfort. That comfort solidifies the trust I have in the value of that relationship.

Likewise, in the most valued relationship of all the ones I have, is that with my *"Daddy."* I have ultimate safety with *"Daddy."* I can be myself without the result or consequence of a false diagnosis. *"Daddy"* will never falsely diagnose me because of one, two, or three off days. He made me; He formed me in my mother's inward parts, so He knows me better than I know myself. Therefore, I could not have enough *"bad days"* for "Daddy" to conclude, *"Tonja, you've changed."* No, *"Daddy"* would love on me, comfort me and tell me to get back to who I really am. Then, He would help me do that which He required. Being with *"Daddy"* is the ultimate comfort and safe place.

Whenever I am "away" from Him, I feel vulnerable.

1. **There was a time when I was far "away" from *"Daddy.*"** **Colossians 1:21** (NLT) - *"This includes you who were once far away from God. You were his enemies, separated from him by your evil thoughts and actions."*

I was vulnerable to the enemy's attacks on my life. I fell into the hands of an abuser. I was subject to backbiting, gossip, and false accusations. I was an enemy of God because I had thoughts that were not of Him. I carried out actions that were not of Him. I did not represent my *"Daddy"* at all. How could I? I did not know Him; I did not spend time with Him. I had been to His house many times, even sensed His presence nearby, but I was never officially introduced to Him. I most certainly did not have the awareness that I was His daughter! The enemy was very skillful and cunning in keeping that awareness from me for years.

2. **After officially meeting *"Daddy,"* at first, it felt like visitation rights. Hebrews 10:39** (NLT) - *"But we are not like those who turn away from God to their own destruction. We are the faithful ones, whose souls will be saved."*

When I first began to know *"Daddy,"* it was difficult to see me the way He wanted me to. It was difficult to believe I was all the things He was showing me I was. So there were times I did not look like the daughter He was revealing to me. There were times during this *"getting to know Daddy season"* that I looked back and wondered if I was who *"they"* said I was. I wondered if the Tonja of yesterday was the real me after all because I was not sure about what was ahead of me. I did not know what was really in that future *"Daddy"* was showing me. He did not give me everything all at once. In His wisdom, He gave me parts at a time, so I could handle each step I needed to take. But in the areas and parts of the unknown that He did not reveal, I would, at times, develop an uncertainty about my future. I would wonder, not so much as to *"WHAT is Daddy not telling me?"* I would wonder, *"WHY is Daddy not telling me?"* In these times of uncertainty, which I know now is a lack of trust in Him and His love for me, I would turn away to look back at the *"me"* I was leaving behind. I was like the *Children of Israel* wanting to return to Egypt to that which was familiar. Even though it was difficult and abusing, painful and torturous, it was familiar, yet the same. It was what I knew. I had become skilled at navigating through the pain. Looking back is a type of turning away. If you are looking back, you are turning away from that which is in front of you. I looked back at times because the future was too uncertain, and it felt uncomfortable, but *"Daddy"* would not have it. Once He had me, He was not going to let me go. He told me, *"I will never leave you, nor forsake you"* (See Hebrews 13:5 - KJV). In His patient way, He helped me to stop looking away from Him because I became vulnerable to the lies each time I did.

3. **Now, I stay very close to His presence. – Psalm 34:18** (NLT) - *"The Lord is close to the brokenhearted; he rescues those whose spirits are crushed."*

Sometimes, people still hurt my feelings and/or treat me unfairly, but *"Daddy"* is always right there.

> **Psalm 145:18** (NLT) – *"The Lord is close to all who call on him, yes, to all who call on him in truth."*

I love *"Daddy"* so much. He reigns the truth in my heart. Therefore, every time I call on Him, He is already there because He is ever-present with me, even in those times when it does not feel like it.

> **Nahum 1:7** (NLT) - *"The Lord is good, a strong refuge when trouble comes. He is close to those who trust in him."*

Jesus told us that as long as we are in this world, we are going to have or face trouble because the world hates us (See *John 15:19*). When I face trouble, *"Daddy"* is always close because I trust Him. I trust Him to be my refuge. Therefore, He is my refuge.

> **Luke 20:25** (NLT) - *"Well then," he said, "give to Caesar what belongs to Caesar, and give to God what belongs to God."*

Time belongs to *"Daddy."* He created time, then He gave us time. Only He knows the times and seasons to come for us (See *Acts 1:7*). All of my time in the day belongs to *"Daddy."* He gives me twenty-four hours daily to grow and accomplish His purpose for me on the earth. I make time out of each twenty-four hours to spend some of

His given time on Him. I make time to be near Him in intimacy, in worship. I make time for studying His Word and learning more of Him. I make time to be taught in the Word by attending His house of prayer weekly. I make time to give back to *"Daddy"* what belongs to Him: TIME.

There are times I have to look away in order to revisit the past, but only for the purpose of giving a testimony. Then I cannot wait to get back in *"Daddy's"* presence again.

GET OUT YOUR JOURNALS:

Who in your company of people makes you feel safe? Why?

- a) Who in your company does not make you feel safe?
- b) What about that person makes you feel safe?
- c) Are you closer to God than you were a few years ago?
- d) How has life gotten safer for you since you have been closer to God?

Chapter 13
Running The Family Business

*E*ventually, I came to the point that I pondered, now that I know who I am and who I belong to; now that I know the *"What"* and the *"Who"*; next, I needed to find out the *"Do."* I had known enough about Daddy over the years to know He had this whole *"Master Plan"* thing going on. This *"Master Plan"* was for the purpose of redeeming. I knew Daddy was in the **Business** of redeeming and restoring. I knew it was a big business, and I knew Daddy was pretty serious about His business. I had seen Him in action a few times on behalf of those I knew and did not know. I saw that Daddy is extremely kind, gentle, and patient. I have seen Him endure a bad reputation about things He had nothing to do with. Sometimes His name was cleared, and many times it was not. But Daddy did not dwell on petty things; He was solely focused on the *"***Business***"* at hand. He told me once, *"Tonja, don't sweat the small stuff. It's about the bigger picture. If you spend too much time nursing the petty matters, you will remain at a petty level and never accomplish the bigger picture."* To ensure I was on the same page, I asked, *"Daddy,* what is the *bigger picture?"* He simply said to me, *"The bigger picture is always about the kingdom, My kingdom."*

Becoming Daddy's Little Girl

"Hmmmmm," I pondered. That helps, but what does that REALLY mean?

Whenever I am in my classroom, and my students begin to get out-of-hand or a bit rambunctious, I announce a reminder to my students that *"This classroom is MY kingdom."* When I make that statement to my students, it means the following:

1. I expect that classroom to reflect my expectations for behavior.

2. I expect the "citizens" of that classroom to conduct themselves according to the rules and expectations of that classroom.

3. I expect that classroom to be a place of safety for my students, the "citizens," to feel free to express themselves without ridicule.

Well, if I take it from that viewpoint, I get it. I get what *"Daddy"* means when He says the *"Bigger Picture"* is about His kingdom.

1. *"Daddy"* expects His kingdom to reflect His expectations for behavior.

2. *"Daddy"* expects the "citizens" of His kingdom to conduct themselves according to the rules and expectations of His kingdom.

3. *"Daddy"* expects His kingdom to be a place of safety for His children to feel free to express themselves without ridicule.

I am an English/Language Arts/Reading teacher. When you can get the reader to make connections, comprehension will begin to manifest. Making a connection is key to understanding the concept you are trying to teach. So when I began to make connections in order to get an understanding of this concept *"Daddy"* needed me to understand, I started to see the picture. Well, I should say this is the picture I started to see. *"Daddy"* established the earth. He then made man in His own image (See Genesis 1:26). He created male and female, then blessed them and said, *"Be fruitful and multiply. Fill the earth and govern it."* (See Genesis 1:27-28). That was the original plan. Somewhere along the way, things got all messed up. *"Daddy"* wanted things back to the way He designed them, but being a God of decency and order, principles and free will, and above all things, a God of love, "Daddy" needed to make that happen without making Himself look bad. He had to play by His own rules, or it would look as if He is a player with bad sportsmanship, holding a grudge, and manipulating the game and rules so He could win. Being the sovereign *"Daddy"* that He is, *"Daddy"* had already come up with a plan to get that done without compromising His standards, character, and loving nature. This plan would allow Him to restore what was lost in His original design. *"Daddy"* is going to win in the end but not through manipulation; He is going to win through love. It has to be love because that is who *"Daddy"* is (See 1 John 4:8). *"Daddy"* is Love. Everything He does is out of the vastness of love that is the essence of who He is. *"Daddy"* is love; He is in the *"**Business**"* of love and loving. Being His child, I have to learn how to run the family *"**Business**.*" I have to learn how to restore what is His and do it all through love. Understanding this *"Bigger Picture"* was the key to me learning how to run the *"Family Business."*

RECAP

1. *"Daddy"* has a master plan for redeeming and restoring His kingdom design back to its original plan.

2. His original plan is so significant and imperative that every response, thought, and decision must be centered on that master plan.

3. All I *"Do"* must be done in the context of **LOVE**.

The Manual

When *"Daddy"* told me He had called me into the family business, being able to effectively assist Him in His master plan seemed impossible to me. But with *"Daddy,"* all things are possible. He makes it possible by supplying me with everything I need to get the job done. The main way He does this is by giving me the *"Manual"* and always allowing me to take an open-book test. *"Daddy"* supplied a book that tells me everything I need to do to be successful at whatever He has purposed me to do. That book is my manual to *"Do"* the *"Family Business"* successfully. That book is called *The Holy Bible*.

Whenever you get hired to work, there is usually an orientation process you must complete. The orientation covers the company's standards and expectations, such as dress code, working hours, benefits, and job duties. Also, for new hires, a training video may be involved. You may be assigned a mentor who does on-the-job training for the new hire. The new hire may remain with the trainer until he or she has mastered their skill set for the company and can perform the job duties independently.

The Assigned Mentor/Trainer

"Daddy" assigned me a mentor to begin my on-the-job training. Unlike the corporate or the secular world, *"Daddy's"* mentor never leaves or forsakes you, even when you have mastered a particular skill set. In *"Daddy's"* manual, or *The Holy Bible*, His mentor is referred to as *"The Helper"* or *"The Comforter." "The Helper"* is with you always; He is the third person of the Trinity, and He lives in you, bringing with Him everything that He is: the *power* of God.

Romans 8:11 (NLT) - *"The Spirit of God, who raised Jesus from the dead, **lives in you**. And just as God raised Christ Jesus from the dead, he will give life to your mortal bodies by **this same Spirit living within you**. (emphasis mine).*

With *"The Helper"* comes *power*; that *power* is to *"Help"* me accomplish my *"Do"* for the kingdom. Whatever *"Daddy"* has called, designed, purposed, or gifted me to *"Do," "The Helper"* has come to live **in me** so I can have the ***power*** to get my **"do"** done. Knowing I have this ***"power"*** from a super-being like my *"Daddy"* gives me the confidence to carry out any assignment I am given.

Becoming Engrained In The Company

One stereotype of a "Daddy's Little Girl" is that of being arrogant. Synonyms for *"arrogant"* are *conceited* or self-important, egotistical, or self-centered. Well, I can see how it can look like that when you are totally convinced of your Daddy's ability and willingness to guarantee your success at whatever you set your mind to accomplish. It could easily be perceived as being arrogant or conceited. Those are worldly terms. When you are the *"Daddy's Little Girl"* of a sovereign God, there is only one word for all of those synonyms: "CONFIDENCE."

1 John 5:14-15 (NLT) - *"And we are **confident** that he hears us whenever we ask for anything that **pleases** him. And since we know he hears us when we make our requests, we also know that he will give us what we ask for." (emphasis mine).*

How can I not be **confident,** knowing that whenever I make a request from my *"Daddy,"* it **will** be given to me? How can I not be confident knowing that whatever I say, I will see it manifest in *"Daddy's"* perfect timing for me? *"Daddy"* works all things together for my good. Whenever I request something, I keep working my *"Do"* within the *"Family Business,"* knowing that the only reason I may be waiting for my request to manifest is because *"Daddy"* is maneuvering everything and everyone involved in bringing that request to reality. In the maneuvering process, *"Daddy"* may encounter someone who is not *"willing"* to be obedient as a participant in His maneuver to bring my request to reality. Being a God of free-will, *"Daddy"* is not going to override someone's free-will. Therefore, when He encounters someone who is not *"willing,"* He has to re-route to encounter an individual who will carry out that part of the plan. He keeps doing this until He gets a *"yes"* from all parties involved. At the end of this process is my answered prayer.

"Daddy" started working on the request as soon as I made it. However, the wait time may have been because of unwilling free-

wills involved in bringing it to past. *"Daddy'* could override their free-will, but He would not because that is not the way He designed the original plan. What we do for Him, He wants it to be because we want to, not because we were made to. If that is the case, *"Daddy"* could have just made puppets in the original design, but He did not do that. He made man in His own image and gave them free-will. When I make a request that pleases Him, I am confident that I am going to get it. Notice the scripture in the *"manual"* says, *"...whenever we ask for anything that pleases Him..."* (See 1 John 5:14 - NLT). How do I know that what I am asking for pleases Him? I have asked that question so many times. I spend so much time with *"Daddy"* and in His *"manual"* that I have learned what pleases Him.

Romans 8:5-8 (NLT) - *"Those who are dominated by the sinful nature think about sinful things, but those who are controlled by the **Holy Spirit** think about things that **please** the Spirit. So letting your sinful nature control your mind leads to death. But letting the Spirit control your mind leads to life and peace. For the sinful nature is always hostile to God. It never did obey God's laws, and it never will. That's why **those who are still under the control of their sinful nature can never please God.**" (emphasis mine).*

Can you imagine never being able to please God? I cannot imagine never being able to please *"Daddy."*

I had to make a decision to come out of the sinful nature that ruled my existence at the time. I had to learn how to be successful at living this holy life *"Daddy"* required me to live. That was a major part of my *"Do."* Remember earlier when I told you *"Daddy"* gave me the *"manual"* and *"The Helper"* to guarantee my success? Well, let us read a little more in Romans 8 to show you how that works.

Growing In Favor In The Business

Romans 8:9,11a,14 (NLT) – *"But you are not controlled by your sinful nature.* ***You are controlled by the Spirit if you have the Spirit of God living in you.*** *(And remember that those who do not have the Spirit of Christ living in them do not belong to him at all.) The Spirit of God, who raised Jesus from the dead, lives in you.* ***For all who are led by the Spirit of God are*** <u>***children of God.***</u>" (emphasis mine).

Did you see it? I knew what I had to do. I had to allow the Holy Spirit living within me to rule my existence. Because I was *"Daddy's Little Girl,"* I had the Holy Spirit living within me, and with the Holy Spirit came the **power** of God to live that holy life He required. Living that holy lifestyle pleased *"Daddy."*

Being a parent myself, I know that whenever a child pleases a parent, no reason is needed to be good to that child. The parent may even invent reasons to be good to that child. When that child asks for anything, there is nothing that the parent will withhold from that child. *"Daddy"* brought this concept to my reality during an experience I had with my three daughters.

My oldest, Jasmine, and my youngest, Donalyn, always felt like my middle daughter, Ashley, was the favored child. The girls and I were all together one day eating out, and the conversation sparked again about Ashley being the *"Favored One."* I asked, *"Why have you two always said that? I don't treat Ashley any different than I treat the two of you."* Then my final gavel statement went down, *"I love all of you the same."* Immediately, figuratively speaking, Jasmine and Donalyn jumped on me with both feet. They began to express the extra perks and benefits that Ashley received that they were not privy to. For the life of me, I could not understand where, how or when they conceived that mindset from my parenting of three beautiful young ladies whom I passionately love equally.

Ashley never helped the situation. She would proudly boast, *"You know I'm Mom's favorite."* Ashley held on to that, even after rebuke. I would say, *"Ashley! Stop encouraging that mindset in your sisters!"* Ashley would calmly respond, *"Well, mom, I am your favorite."* For weeks, months, and years after that, I could not understand how we got there. One day, I was in my kitchen when *"The Helper"* brought it all to a place of understanding for me. It was like watching a movie. I saw that no matter what I asked Ashley to do or required of her throughout the years, she would do it without hesitation and without resistance. Her sisters were the total opposite; they were rebellious and stubborn. Jasmine was a quiet rebel, never disrespectful. She would hear me and may even respond, *"Yes, mam,"* but because she had no intentions of complying with my request, she would just not do what I asked, or it would be a case of her going and doing what she wanted to do anyway. Donalyn, the baby girl, was a little more vocal than Jasmine. Often, Donalyn would voice her disapproval of my request or challenge *"Why"* she was being asked to do that thing or she would procrastinate at getting it done, if she did it at all. I look at her today and am amazed that she still has a full set of teeth in her mouth. Then *"The Helper"* began to show me that whenever I went to the store, Ashley was considered in my purchases because I wanted to reward her for her obedience. It is a parent's way.

Deuteronomy 12:28 (NLT) - *"Be careful to **obey** all my commands, so that all will go well with you and your children after you, because* *you will be doing what is good and pleasing to the LORD your God." (emphasis mine).*

Deuteronomy 28:1-2 (NLT) - *"If you **fully obey** the LORD your God and carefully keep all his commands that I am giving you today, the LORD your God will set you high above all the nations of the world. **You will experience all these blessings if you obey the LORD your God.**" (emphasis mine).*

It is a parent's way. It is ingrained in a parent to reward a child for obedience. God made us in His image. Some things we *"Do"* just like He does because it is the way we are. We were made like Him in those ways. Even sinful parents do the same thing; even more so is a Godly parent going to reward a child for obedience.

Matthew 7:11 (NLT) - *"So if you sinful people know how to give good gifts to your children, how much more will your heavenly Father give good gifts to those who ask him."*

I have learned, and I am putting into practice what pleases *"Daddy"* - OBEDIENCE. I have learned so much of *"Daddy"* that my free-will has become merged with His will. Therefore, I want what He wants because whatever I ask for is what He wants to give me anyway. I know without a doubt that I will get what I ask for. Although there are still times I ask the question if what I am asking for is pleasing to Him. When my request is so personal, I cannot find it anywhere in the *"manual."* In the wait, I may wonder if my request is pleasing to *"Daddy."* Then I stand on the part in the *"manual"* that tells me *"Daddy"* wants to give me my heart's desires because of my obedience; I then regain my confidence.

RECAP

My *"Do"* is to be **obedient** and live a life of holiness before a sinful world. *"The Helper"* living within me empowers me with the **power of God** to guarantee my success.

This fits into *"Daddy's"* master plan because my holy living will draw others to Him. This is significant because it is *"Daddy's"* will that all be saved. That is why He sent Jesus to die on the cross for sin once and for all.

Titus 2:11-12 (NLT) - *"For the grace of God has been revealed, bringing salvation to all people. And we are **instructed** to turn from godless living and sinful pleasures. **We should live in this evil world with wisdom, righteousness, and devotion to God.**" (emphasis mine).*

We can "Do" this with *"The Helper"* living in us and giving us the **power of God** to walk in wisdom, righteousness, and devotion to God. What does this kind of holy living look like? What is the point of this kind of holy living? Well, my friend, this kind of holy living is rolled out very specifically in the *"manual."* This kind of holy living empowers you to affect and influence the lives of those around you. This kind of holy living empowers you to impact the lives of others and lead them to make decisions that will bring them into Godly kingdom living. Let us look at a few promises from the *"manual."*

Holy Living Empowers You:

1. <u>**To give the right response.**</u> **Colossians 4:6** (NLT) - *"Let your conversation be gracious and attractive so that you will have the right response for everyone."*

As you grow in favor in the kingdom, while you are at work, home, the grocery store, out shopping, or even at the doctor's office, you may run into someone who wants to tell you about their problems, sickness, challenges, issues and the like. You want to give that person the right response, right? You never want someone to leave you feeling worse off than when they first came to you. *"Daddy'* wants us to make a difference in the lives of others, a good difference. We represent *"Daddy"* while we are here on earth. Therefore, we should *"Do"* as He would *"Do"* if He were here on earth. Always having the right words to say is what *"Daddy"* would have. Therefore, His children should always have the right words as well. Jesus represented *"Daddy"* while He was on the earth, and Jesus always had the right words to say, even in times of anger. You need the **power** that comes with *"The Helper"* living inside you to accomplish this *"Do."*

2. <u>**To give encouragement to those who need it.**</u> **Ephesians 4:29** (NLT) - *"Don't use foul or abusive language. Let everything you say be good and helpful, so that your words will be an encouragement to those who hear them."*

This can be difficult for me at times. There are moments I need the **POWER** of God to keep me from using abusive language. When I am able to keep myself in those moments, I am confident that "The Helper" is with me and gives me the power to represent "Daddy" positively. I hate the thought of giving people the right to say that famous line of judgment, *"And she's supposed to be a Christian."* I AM A CHRISTIAN. Even Christians have their *"bad"* days but not when the world is looking on. You are not allowed to have a bad day because your one bad day cancels out all your good days, and it makes *"Daddy"* look bad; it gives Him a bad reputation. That is why we have to allow *"The Helper"* to help us with the inward challenges. You need the **power** that comes with *"The Helper"* living inside you to accomplish this *"Do."*

3. <u>**To patiently love someone through a difficult time.**</u> James 1:19 (NLT) - *"Understand this, my dear brothers and sisters: You must all be quick to listen, slow to speak, and slow to get angry."*

Have you ever heard the saying, *"I just put my foot in my mouth?"* Well, I believe that comes from not being able to carry out this *"Do"* from the *"manual."* There were so many times I said something that I had to apologize for or something I wish I could take back. I may have misunderstood what was going on, jumped to a conclusion, got angry or hurt and said some words in defense or to cover up my pain. Later, when I found out the *"real"* story, I wish I had not said what I said. That will not happen if we are slow to speak, slow to get angry, and most of all, quick to listen. I have gotten a lot better at listening, but there are times I still need to work on being slow to speak and slow to get angry. You need the **power** that comes with *"The Helper"* living inside you to accomplish this *"Do."*

4. <u>**To be kind like God and turn others from their sin.**</u> **Romans 2:4** (NLT) - *"Don't you see how wonderfully kind, tolerant, and patient God is with you? Does this mean*

nothing to you? Can't you see that his kindness is intended to turn you from your sin?"

This level of kindness requires the **power** of God! When *"Daddy"* began to work this *"kindness"* into my *"Do,"* He would bring the most difficult people on earth to take me through these practices. It used to be so hard for me to be tolerant of a mean person. It used to be extremely challenging for me to be patient with a person who keeps doing the same stupid things repeatedly, even after you have given them sound, solid, Godly counsel about that matter. The worse one for me was a person who was knowingly in sin but kept nursing that sin with excuses because he or she did not want to give it up. When my training in this area came up, and it often did, *"The Help*er" had to continually remind me that *"Daddy"* was just as patient with me while He desired me to come out of my sin. That reminder would always bring me down a peg. I knew *"Daddy"* was more patient with me than I could ever be with someone else. I was a piece of work! I would always tease my New Orleans pastor and say, "*God put him on overtime duty when He brought me through the doors of his church.*" You need the **power** that comes with *"The Helper"* living inside you to accomplish this *"Do."*

5. **To be humble and put others first.** Philippians 2:3-5 (NLT) - *Don't be selfish; don't try to impress others. Be humble, thinking of others as better than yourselves. Don't look out only for your own interests, but take an interest in others, too. You must have the same attitude that Christ Jesus had."*

I love watching the show *"Forensic Files,"* or shows that involve forensics. When solving certain crimes, the coroner would look for defensive wounds to determine if the victim had put up a fight. I learned through these shows that it is in our nature to automatically respond in defense when danger is detected. That is why we blink when something suddenly comes toward our face; the body is defending the safety of the eyes. That is why we put our arms up if someone is swinging something or throwing something towards us; our body is protecting and defending against that incoming object. Knowing this makes me understand the requirement of this segment in the *"manual."* If your body is designed to look out for itself when danger is detected automatically, you will need the **power** of *"The Helper"* to be able to put others before yourself. When you are working hard, trying to make ends meet to provide for your family, it can be difficult to take an interest in others. But all things are possible with *"Daddy."* He gives you everything you need to be successful to live the way He wants you to. He gives you the ability and strength to be able to put others before yourself. You need the **power** that comes from *"The Helper"* living inside you to accomplish this *"Do."*

6. **To not judge outwardly, but to look at the heart. 1 Samuel 16:7** (NLT) - *But the LORD said to Samuel, "Don't judge by his appearance or height, for I have rejected him. The LORD doesn't see things the way you see them. People judge by outward appearance, but the LORD looks at the heart."*

I have done a lot of repenting when it came to walking out this part of my *"Do."* I lost track of how many times I confessed to someone that I misjudged them when they initially came across my path. It is still happening. Just recently, I worked in the same building with a particular co-worker. Of course, I had seen her passing through the hallway, in the same staff meetings, and coming and going to various areas in the building. We had many opportunities to speak to each other and did just that, but that was all. I only knew her on the surface. I could pick her out of a crowd by name, but I did not really know her. Even though I did not know her, I had subconsciously categorized who I thought she was.

During the next school year of 2017-2018, she and I were working at the same grade level. This presented opportunities for us to be in each other's company over a period of time. I discovered that I really enjoyed her company. She had a wonderful sense of humor and was very down-to-earth. I confessed to her that I thought she was not someone I would enjoy being around. In this case, I was the poster child for judging a book by the cover. This part of the "*manual*" tells us not to judge based on outward appearances; judge according to the heart. That takes getting to know a person beyond what they look like.

Getting to know a person takes time, so if you are drawing conclusions without giving someone the time to reveal their true self, you may be judging according to outward appearance; you may not be judging according to knowledge. Allow time and the Holy Spirit living within you to reveal that person's true self. You need the **power** that comes with "*The Helper*" living inside you to accomplish this "*Do*."

7. **To gain complete knowledge of His will. Colossians 1:9** (NLT) - *"So we have not stopped praying for you since we first heard about you. We ask God to give you complete knowledge of his will ..."*

How different would life be if you had complete knowledge of God's will for your life? What would your *"To Do"* list for the week look like, knowing God's will for you and that nothing you do toward His will can fail? If you can begin to write down some things you would do differently, or if you can write down how different you would be, that means you are not there yet. It is okay; I am not there either. I cannot say I know the *complete* will of God for me. I know a lot more about His will for me now than a few years ago, but it is not complete. I have to really trust the Holy Spirit living within me for that knowledge on an ongoing basis as I make decisions, respond to other people and react to life's circumstances, among other things. Because I am not convinced of *"Daddy's"* complete will for me when things happen, I have to depend on *"The Comforter"* to tell me what to do. *"The Comforter"* knows what my complete will is. That is why *"Daddy"* assigned *"The Comforter"* to me for all my days on earth.

"The Comforter" knows what I am supposed to *"Do"* here on earth. He knows everything: every blessing and every moment that *"Daddy"* has planned for me. I do not know, so sometimes I get things wrong; sometimes I mess things up, and sometimes I think I know what is best for me, and I react and make decisions based on what I think I am sure of, and I screw it up. But have no fear! *"The Comforter"* is so awesome. He is patient and kind; He is always there to work out those mess-ups for me and get me back to where *"Daddy"* designed me to be. Even though I do not know *"Daddy's"* complete will for me yet, as long as I have *"The Comforter,"* I have *"Daddy's"* complete will for me. Therefore, I will accomplish every good thing *"Daddy"* has willed for my life. I am confident of that. You can walk confidently in that complete knowledge for your life

as well. You need the **power** that comes with *"The Helper"* living inside you to accomplish this *"Do."*

8. **To gain spiritual wisdom and understanding**. **Colossians 1:9** (NLT) - *"So we have not stopped praying for you since we first heard about you. We ask God to give you ... spiritual wisdom and understanding..."*

When I became engrafted in the *"company"* (kingdom), it was very important for me to operate in wisdom. If I did not operate in wisdom, I could mess everything up and cause a soul to turn from *"Daddy"* instead of winning a soul for Him. Understanding matters was equally important. Proverbs 4:7 (KJV) tells us that *"Wisdom is the principal thing; therefore, get wisdom; and with all thy getting get understanding."* In our day-to-day dealings on the earth, I must learn to handle my matters with wisdom and understanding. I cannot afford to be foolish. Gaining wisdom and understanding empowers me to walk in the **power** of my weapons to win others to Christ. In doing so, I can change their human reasoning and false arguments from being against *"Daddy"* to being for *"Daddy"* and, in turn, change their behavior from being disobedient to *"Daddy"* to willingly obeying *"Daddy."* Look at 2 Corinthians 10:4-5.

2 Corinthians 10:4-5 (NLT) *"We use God's mighty weapons, not worldly weapons, to knock down the strongholds of human reasoning and to destroy false arguments. We destroy every proud obstacle that keeps people from knowing God. We capture their rebellious thoughts and teach them to obey Christ."*

I cannot do any of this without wisdom and understanding; the wisdom and understanding that comes through holy living; the holy living that can be achieved successfully through the **power** of the Holy Spirit within us. You need the p**ower** that comes with *"The Helper"* living inside you to accomplish this *"Do."*

9. **To live in a way that honours and pleases the Lord. Colossians 1:9a-10a** (NLT) - *"So we have not stopped praying for you since we first heard about you. .... Then the way you live will always honor and please the Lord..."*

The kind of living that honours and pleases the Lord is holy living. The way to begin and continue to practice holy living is to always allow yourself and/or your awareness to be controlled by the Holy Spirit. Do you remember Romans 8:5? When you allow the Holy Spirit to control your thoughts, decisions, and actions, He will always lead you into doing what pleases God. He will not MAKE you do it. That will go against *"Daddy's"* original design. However, He will make it pretty clear what you need to do to please God. It is then up to your free-will to choose to be OBEDIENT and carry out what the Holy Spirit is leading you to do. You need the **power** that comes with *"The Helper"* living inside you to accomplish this *"Do."*

10. **To produce every kind of good fruit. Colossians 1:9-10** (NLT) - *"So we have not stopped praying for you since we first heard about you. ... and your lives will produce every kind of good fruit. ..."*

Let me make sure you know that this portion of scripture is NOT saying you are going to plant a garden and begin to produce apples, oranges, and pears. The fruit mentioned here is the spiritual fruit that God produces. You will find those fruit listed in Galatians 5:22. The fruit of the Spirit is love, joy, peace, patience, kindness,

85

goodness, and faithfulness. It is very difficult to produce some of these fruits. However, with the Holy Spirit empowering you to live a holy life that pleases God, you and others will definitely see all of these good fruits coming out of your lifestyle. You need the **power** that comes with *"The Helper"* living inside you to accomplish this *"Do."*

> *11.* **To grow and learn God better and better. Colossians 1:9-10** (NLT) – *"So we have not stopped praying for you since we first heard about you. ... you will grow as you learn to know God better and better."*

Learning God better and better makes living for Him easier and easier. The more you know Him, the more of Him you will allow inside of you. The more God resides in you, is the more **power He** imparts to you and empowers you to live a life that is pleasing to Him, and you as well. When you know you are living for God, it builds confidence in your existence. You can know you are making a difference in someone's life on the earth. Knowing God better and better makes you want to please Him more and more. Pleasing Him more and more makes God want to bless you more and more. I love pleasing *"Daddy,"* not because He blesses me but because He is pleased with me. I love to please *"Daddy"* because I love the way it makes me feel. I love knowing I can please a sovereign God. It **empowers** me to know that what I am doing in that moment is pleasing an almighty God. For example, let us say someone has just made me very angry and I want to speak my anger or, as I used to say, *"give them a piece of my mind,"* but *"The Comforter"* says, *"Hold your peace. Your 'Daddy' is working on this one."* When I stand there and do not say anything in my obedience to *"The Comforter,"* I feel such **power** within me at that moment, knowing

I am doing what is pleasing to my *"Daddy."* You can know that feeling too. You need the **power** that comes with *"The Helper"* living inside you to accomplish this *"Do."*

> *12.* **To live a Godly life.** 2 Peter 1:3 (NLT) - *"By his **divine power**, God has given us everything we need for living a godly life. We have received all of this by coming to know him, the one who called us to himself by means of his marvelous glory and excellence." (emphasis mine).*

At this point in my life, my priority is to please God. Whether in my decisions, actions, responses, thoughts, desires, or whatever concerns my existence, I want my *"Daddy"* to be happy with whatever I *"Do."* The only way I can guarantee that is by living a holy life. The only way I can guarantee that I will live a holy life is to depend on **the power** within me; that **power** that comes with having the Holy Spirit living **inside of me**. This power residing in me empowers me to know *"Daddy"* in a personal way; it empowers me to know *"Daddy's"* complete will for my life; it empowers me to live a life that represents the character and personality of God, my *"Daddy."* The Holy Spirit empowers me to *"Do"* what Jesus did while here on earth, and that is to show the world the love of the sovereign Father. We can *"Do"* it. You need the **power** that comes with *"The Helper"* living inside you to accomplish this *"Do."*

Receiving Your Assignment

Once you have completed your on-the-job training, you are ready to begin the next stage of running the family business. That one-on-one time with your mentor is no longer necessary. During your training or probationary segment, your mentor was there at every step. You almost could not go to the restroom without that person being there, but not anymore. Now that you have been tried, tested, and trained, you have proven that you can fulfill your company obligations on your own.

While you were with your trainer, your work experience was through his or her assignments. You learned how to do the job through the responsibilities that the trainer had, based on that trainer's assignment. But after your probationary period and on-the-job training, you have proven that you are ready for your own assignment. Your first solo assignment may be different from what you were doing during the training season. As you were proven with that one assignment, you may be given another, or God may shift you to a different assignment, bringing more challenges that become opportunities for you to grow.

When I got to this point, *"Daddy"* gave me my own personal assignment. I was assigned to Sunday School Teacher. Then as I continued to grow in that position and proved myself as a committed follower and teacher of Jesus Christ and *"Daddy's"* company, I was assigned to teach new members. That assignment led to me being assigned to teach the ministers of the church. I loved it. I loved every minute of getting the lessons prepared; I loved facilitating the classes; I loved it all. *"Daddy"* continued to make life interesting and challenging, always giving me a reason to wake up and look forward to another day of purpose and fulfillment. *"Daddy"* was grooming me for my ultimate *"Do"* in the family business, the kingdom. I know now my *"Do"* is to teach. I teach through various vehicles, but they all involve teaching. I must remember, though, in all I "Do," I must "Do" it in LOVE. You need the **power** that comes with *"The Helper"* living inside you to accomplish this *"Do."*

Always Accepting New Applicants

If you are reading this book or even just this chapter and you have not made the decision to accept *"Daddy's"* plan for abundant life, I invite you to do so now. *"Daddy"* wants to be good to everyone, but He will not override your free-will. He wants you, but He wants you to want Him too. If you are sick and tired of being sick and tired, try *"Daddy's"* plan. If you are continually feeling empty in your existence even though you have an abundance of *"things,"* try *"Daddy's"* plan. Maybe you were a believer, or are a believer, but you have somehow found yourself having an affair with *"The World."* You believe in *"Daddy's"* plan; you know about the things you have read in this book. However, you go clubbing with your friends, you drink with them, and you curse with them. You give your body to men for sex, and you are not married. You may be giving your body to men or a man for sex, and you are married. I am talking to you as well.

Romans 12:2 (NLT) - *"Don't copy the behavior and customs of this world, but let God transform you into a new person by changing the way you think. Then you will learn to know God's will for you, which is good and pleasing and perfect."*

You may have been a believer for quite some time now, but maybe you are searching for something more. You may have asked yourself, *"Is this it? Is this all to serving a sovereign God?"* Then you concluded, *"There's got to be more."* Well, I will tell you; there is more. I have been in that place where I asked those same questions and determined there has to be more to it than what I have experienced. I say to you now, *"Launch into the deep."* Take the plunge and go deeper into the things of God. There is a *"will"* that *"Daddy"* has designed specifically for you. That will is good and pleasing, and best of all, it is perfect for you.

1 Corinthians 10:13 (NLT) - *"The temptations in your life are no different from what others experience. And God is faithful. He will not allow the temptation to be more than you can stand. When you are tempted, he will show you a way out so that you can endure."*

"Daddy" will show you that way out, but He is not going to make you take it. Remember, He is a God of free-will. You must desire to come out of that temptation. So when He shows you the way out, GO THAT WAY.

Nahum 1:2 (NLT) – *"The LORD is a jealous God, filled with vengeance and rage. He takes revenge on all who oppose him and continues to rage against his enemies!"*

As kind and gentle as *"Daddy"* is, do not mistake the fact that He has another side to Him. *"Daddy"* does get angry. But, do not think of *"Daddy's"* enemies as a person. *"Daddy"* does not hate people; He hates the *"acts"* that people do.

Proverbs 6:16-19 (NLT) – *"There are six things the LORD hates—no, seven things he detests: haughty eyes, a __lying__ tongue, hands that __kill__ the innocent, a heart that __plots__ evil, feet that __race__ to do wrong, a false witness who __pours__ out lies, a person who __sows__ discord in a family." (emphasis mine).*

I highlighted the verbs for you. The verbs are the *"**acts**"* that *"Daddy"* hates. We make the mistake of assigning our dislike to a person. Yes, that person made the decision to carry out the *"act,"* but if that person no longer did those *"**acts**"* and began to *"Do"* the things that please *"Daddy,"* we would no longer assign our dislike to that person, so it was not the person we disliked or hated. We hated the *"**acts**"* that person was carrying out. So let us get that part straight from now on. *"The manual"* even says that our battles are not with people (each other); our battles, or fight, is against rulers and wickedness in high places and the unseen world (See Ephesians 6:12). We can see people.

Deuteronomy 4:24 (NLT) - *"The LORD your God is a devouring fire; he is a jealous God."*

Even in **Nahum 1:2**, it mentions that *"Daddy"* is jealous, and here it is again. *"Daddy"* wants all my devotion and loyalty. That is perfectly understandable. If I hired you for my company, I do not want you working for my competitor and me; that is a conflict of interest. I really would not know where or with whom the depths of your loyalties reside. So if we are running *"Daddy's"* family business, He wants sole devotion to the cause.

Consequently, He wants to eradicate any *"**acts**"* that may oppose His mission. Therefore, Nahum and Deuteronomy, in the *"manual,"* tells us how aggressive *"Daddy"* can be with getting rid of those things which can be *"acts"* or *"thoughts"* that would cause us to displease Him and fail at being successful. *"Daddy"* wants you to be successful. He guarantees your success.

You Will Have Full Support Of The Business Plan – You Will Have Super Powers Within You

1 Corinthians 6:19 (NLT) - *"Don't you realize that your body is the temple of **the Holy Spirit**, <u>who lives in you</u> and was given to you by God? You do not belong to yourself,"* (emphasis mine).

Ephesians 3:16-17 (NLT) - *"I pray that from his glorious, unlimited resources **he will empower you** <u>with inner strength</u> through his Spirit. Then Christ will make his home in your hearts as you trust in him. Your roots will grow down into God's love and keep you strong."* (emphasis mine).

Ephesians 3:20 (NLT) - *"Now all glory to God, who is able, through **his mighty power** <u>at work within us</u>, to accomplish infinitely more than we might ask or think."* (emphasis mine).

Colossians 1:11 (NLT) - **"We also pray that you will be strengthened with all his glorious power so you will have all the endurance and patience you need. May you be filled with joy."** (emphasis mine).

You are not too bad to be a *"Daddy's Little Girl."* You have not been so terrible that you are beyond help or healing. You are not too wretched to be saved. Nothing is impossible for *"Daddy"* to *"Do"* something with.

Psalm 72:12-14 (NLT) - *" He will rescue the poor when they cry to him; he will help the oppressed, who have no one to defend them. He feels pity for the weak and the needy, and he will rescue them.*

He will redeem them from oppression and violence, for their lives are precious to him."

"Daddy" is so full of love for you. He is so full of concern for you that He takes it personally when someone else is concerned or not concerned for you.

Proverbs 14:31 (NLT) - *"Those who oppress the poor insult their Maker, but helping the poor honors him."*

We each have our own *"business plan."* Your *"business plan"* is wrapped up in the gift and purpose *"Daddy"* has given you to accomplish while you are here on earth. Your *"business plan"* is the reason "Daddy" formed you in your mother's womb; it is the reason He birthed you on the earth. At your birth, *"Daddy"* enabled you with every natural ability to get that *"business plan"* accomplished. Your acceptance of His Son, Jesus, gives you access to get His ***SUPER*** power applied to that **natural ability** in order to **<u>guarantee</u>** your *"business plan"* is accomplished.

Romans 12:6-8 (NLT) - *"In his grace, God has given us different gifts for doing certain things well. So, if God has given you the ability to prophesy, speak out with as much faith as God has given you. If your gift is serving others, serve them well. If you are a teacher, teach well. If your gift is to encourage others, be encouraging. If it is giving, give generously. If God has given you leadership ability, take the responsibility seriously. And if you have a gift for showing kindness to others, do it gladly."*

If you will accept Jesus as your Lord and Savior, then *"Daddy"* will send *"The Helper"* to live in you and **empower** you to establish your *"business plan"* here on earth. In accepting Jesus as your Lord and Saviour, you will be assisting *"Daddy"* in restoring His original design of the *"Master Plan."* If you have accepted Jesus as your Lord and Savior, then it is my hope that the words of this book have focused you on your *"Do"* in the kingdom design, and you will increase in the **power** that lives in you to *"Do"* even greater works than you have already accomplished.

Becoming a *"Daddy's Little Girl"* was a process I stepped into unknowingly. I love what *"Daddy"* has taught me through that process. I am honored and filled with an overwhelming confidence of *"Daddy's"* love for me. This confidence in His love grows every day and empowers me with the boldness to step out and walk out the design He has intended for my life. It is a wonderful feeling and a wonderful existence. With *"Daddy,"* I am full of life and power. I desire the same for you.

Ephesians 3:18-19 (NLT) - *"And may you have the **power** to understand, as all God's people should, how wide, how long, how high, and how deep his love is. May you experience the love of Christ, though it is too great to understand fully.* **Then you will be made complete <u>with all the fullness of life and power that comes from God.</u>***" (emphasis mine).*

Did you see that? You will have all the fullness of life and all the fullness of power. The best part of this is that the fullness and the power come from God. God is supernatural; therefore, this life and power that comes to you from Him is supernatural as well. You would not be able to accomplish what God wants for you in your natural self. You need His superpower on your natural ability to accomplish and live the life God has designed for you.

The life and power that comes from God is laid out in His Word. God honors His Word. If you speak anything contrary to His Word, He will not move on it. You must speak out of His Word; His Word is His will. When you speak His Word, He will honor it. Therefore, what you speak WILL come to pass. He gives you the Holy Spirit to live in you to help you master how to live out and speak His Word. Then, because the Holy Spirit is there to honor God's Word, the Holy Spirit will bring that Word of God you just spoke into physical manifestation. It is a win-win lifestyle. God's Word tells you how to please Him; therefore, you will have the power to please Him. God's Word tells you how to encourage; therefore, you will have the power to encourage others. God's Word tells you how to turn others from sin; therefore, you will have the power to turn others from sin. God's Word tells you how to be humble; therefore, you will have the power to be humble. God's Word tells you how to judge righteously; therefore, you will have the power to judge righteously.

"*The Comforter*" living in you means that you have the power to do all that God has designed for you to "*Do.*" You have the power to succeed at what God wants for you; you have the power to hold your peace when you need to; you have the power to know when to say "yes" and when to say "no"; and you have the power to respond in ways that please God. You will know because it is in the "*manual.*" You will "Do" it because "*The Comforter*" is there to help you get it done.

"*The Manual*" is His Word, so when you speak His Word, you will see what you speak come to pass. When you speak His Word, "*The Comforter*" begins to move on His Word to bring it to pass. Therefore, what you speak from His Word will manifest in your life. That is what happens when a super God places a super Comforter within you to assist with your natural abilities. Through obedience, you will begin to live a supernatural lifestyle. Walking and talking the Word of God will cause you to see what you say. You will be a true hero for God walking the earth because you will have superpowers. You can do it; you can come out; you can rise up; you can overcome, and you can be victorious. You WILL be victorious because all things are possible with God.

You will have superpowers because God is with you.

Say it with me, "**I have superpowers!**"

I HAVE SUPERPOWERS!

About the Author

Tonja L. Davis is a very prophetic writer. From the saved to the unsaved, her writings paint a practical picture of truth from the principles of God's Word. Her writings are like small seeds that seep through even narrow cracks to find their way to the soil of a person's heart, which eventually produces a harvest of self-revelation. Although Tonja L. Davis has now come into her own revelation of her ideal identity, she does not write from that place. She writes from her broken place, which empowers her writing to resonate with all who read her work. Her gift of transparency is a unique tool that God uses to impact the lives of all who consume her work.

Made in the USA
Columbia, SC
08 July 2024